the witch doesn't drown in this one

also by amanda lovelace

the
women are some kind of magic
poetry series:

the princess saves herself in this one (#1)
the witch doesn't burn in this one (#2)
the mermaid's voice returns in this one (#3)

slay those dragons: a journal for writing your own story

believe in your own magic oracle deck & guidebook

***

the
things that h(a)unt
poetry duology:

to make monsters out of girls (#1)
to drink coffee with a ghost (#2)

***

the
you are your own fairy tale
poetry trilogy:

break your glass slippers (#1)
shine your icy crown (#2)
unlock your storybook heart (#3)

***

flower crowns & fearsome things
(a standalone poetry collection)

***

cozy witch tarot deck
& guidebook

cozy witch tarot coloring book

***

make your own magic: a beginner's guide to
self-empowering witchcraft

your magical journal: a place for self-reflection,
spellwork, & making your own magic

your magical life: a young witch's guide
to becoming happy, confident, & powerful

***

she followed the moon back to herself
(a standalone poetry collection)

***

chubby witch's night in:
a 44-card oracle deck & guidebook

the witch doesn't drown in this one

amanda lovelace

to every woman
who has lost
her fire as well
as her hope—

neither is a
finite resource.
remember that
& keep going, going, going.

trigger warning

intimate partner abuse,
sexual assault,
suicide,
self-harm,
eating disorders,
abortion,*
trauma,
death,
murder,
violence,
guns,
fire,
menstruation,
queerphobia,
misogyny,
transphobia,
& possibly more.

remember to practice self-care
before, during, & after
reading.

*this author & this book are pro-choice, which will be made abundantly clear in the following pages. however, the author recognizes that some might be triggered by the topic of abortion for personal reasons (e.g., unwanted abortion).

note from the author

it all began with a dream—

no, but really, it did. like, actually.

i never planned to write more installments in the women are some kind of magic poetry series. after i published *the princess saves herself in this one* (2017), *the witch doesn't burn in this one* (2018), & *the mermaid's voice returns in this one* (2019), i thought that was it, that i was done with it, give or take a few small projects here & there.

forever.

i moved on to other poetry series—plus some stand-alones—& even into new genres. my first poetry series became something of the past, something i was nostalgic about but knew for certain was finished, especially after publishing the *believe in your own magic* oracle deck (2020), which tied up all the collections with a nice little bow.

then one night i had a dream. it's been a while since then, so the details are a little fuzzy, but in it i had begun writing a companion to *the witch doesn't burn in this one*, the middle book in the series.

sometime the next day, i remember waking up & asking my wife, "wouldn't it be wild if that really happened?"

(yeeeeah, it certainly would be, my past self.)

at first, i thought it was just a normal, run-of-the-mill dream, but it became one of those dreams i could never seem to shake off, not even months later. it stayed with me, constantly whispering in my ear as i worked on other projects, *look closer. pay attention. you're going to miss the moment if you don't.*

when i signed the contract for my most recent poetry collection, *she followed the moon back to herself* (2024), it was actually a two-book contract where the title & concept of the second book were not yet final.

it took a while to decide what i wanted to do. eventually, i landed on the theme of being a sad witch—poetry that was a little less empowering & a little more in my feelings. when i began writing it, i had no intention of it being a companion to *the witch doesn't burn in this one*, but from the first few poems i penned, it was very clear to me that that's what it was. turns out i had a lot to say about the state of the world since 2018, especially when it came to women's issues . . .

funny how things work out, especially if you resist them as much as possible.

you don't need to have read the women are some kind of magic series to read this book (no, not even *the witch doesn't burn in this one*), but if you have, this companion might make for a more meaningful read. either way, i hope *the witch doesn't drown in this one* finds you exactly when you need it.

laced with love,
amanda

contents

caution ahead:

some
stories that

start
with bitch-fire

&

beautiful
woman-passion

end
with tearstains,

but

that
doesn't mean

that
we are weak.

it just means

that we need
to find

new strengths
& strategies.

I. the bitch-fire rages on

she used to
think that
dragon
was an apt
word
to describe
dangerous
& greedy men
who use & abuse
women.

now she
knows that
the real dragons
are the women
who are
ferocious
enough
to
fight against
their oppressors.

—keep breathing your fire, ladies.

i can't help
but to wonder

when these
powerful men

in such
powerful buildings

wielding
powerful pens

will stop
trying to tell me what

i can & can't do
with my own damn body.

—a thing of fairy tales | a dream untrue.

shhh, be quiet a moment.
do you hear that?

that's every goddess
in the universe
screaming out in anger
at the same time.

you better hope
they go easy on you.

—spoiler: they probably won't.

i
am
more
important
than
anything
that may
or may not
blossom
in
the pit
of my
belly.

—fuck your so-called opinion.

you do know that

your
personal values

& your
personal beliefs

do not
apply to anyone

but *you*, right?

—it seems most of you have forgotten.

even
goddess
brigid
once
performed
the miracle
of
abortion

&
she was
so
beloved,
they now
call
her
a saint.

—the more you know.

they
can't exactly
be
called *rights*

if
they can be
stripped
down

to the
marrow
&
fed to

the
firepit
at
any

m
o
m
e
n
t.

—this shit isn't working ~~anymore~~.

women

are not
the only ones

who can give birth.

(on that note,
not every woman can.)

do not forget

that every person
of every gender

deserves to have

comfort, safety,
protection, & choice.

—*inclusivity.*

"believe women,"
they said &
they hashtagged.

—we didn't realize they weren't finished.

"except that one
& that one
& that one."

—it's all women or nothing, assholes.

make sure every
woman's voice is

heard.

—if i have to stand by your side alone, i will.

here's the thing:

if you only
support her
if she's likable

& behaves
perfectly
at all times,

you don't
get to call
yourself

a feminist.

—you're literally just a misogynist in disguise.

just because
you, as a woman,

have yet to

recognize
the ways in which

the patriarchy

has oppressed you
& dimmed your light,

that doesn't mean

that you can't support
the women who are

brave enough

to speak about
their experiences.

—your experience is not every experience.

when i say i'm
a girl's girl,
i mean *every* girl.

every.
single.
one.

*—i've said it before, & i'll say it again:
trans women are women.*

she
doesn't
dress
hoping
she
looks
pretty
to some
man.

—how embarrassing of
you to think so.

she
dresses
like
she’s
preparing
to go
into
fucking
battle.

—after all, every day
feels like one.

do not be fooled,
as the history books

often
get it wrong

& it's not
an accident.

you are *not*
a born nurturer.

you are *not*
a born gatherer.

what they don't
want you to know is,

plenty of women
were hunters, too.

you can provide
everything for yourself.

—gender roles were made up by man & benefit only him.

so what
if
it's her
dream

to
live
& laugh
& love?

i don't
blame
her
one bit.

she can
barely do
any of
those things

without
looking
over her
shoulder

to see
if it's too
dangerous
first.

—leave her alone.

"woman—
hold nothing back,

for when they
called you a serpent,

they didn't realize
they were giving you

permission to
unleash your venom."

—*lilith II.*

you really think
we were made
from adam's rib?

that's
adorable.

i, too, believed in
fairy tales
for way too long.

*—god is a woman & she made us from
everything sacred.*

"your poetry
reads as if
it's the diary
of an angsty
teenage girl."

first of all,

there's
absolutely
nothing
wrong with
teenage girls.

second of all,

no shit—
who do you
think i've been
writing for
this entire time?

—my inner teenager, who's finally allowed to say how she feels.

she
hasn't
just
walked
through
the fires
of hell
&
survived.

—that woman is hell itself without any encouragement from a man.

men think
domestic violence

jokes
are funny because

they are
convinced that

women are
the punchline

to every joke
that's ever been told.

—they don't care about our pain.

my roman empire—

the nightmare that
keeps me up at all hours—

is the fact that
our bodies are not safe

from male
consumption

even when we are dead.

—they will never let us rest.

every girl
in
this bar
has a
medusa
tattoo—

you
know
what
that
means,
right?

it
means
that
they're all
ruthless
survivors,

so i
wouldn't
try
anything
if i were
you.

—they go as hard as stone.

the other day
i heard
a man say
that
they should
make divorce
illegal again

so
no woman
will ever
be able to
fuck him over,
do whatever
she wants.

(goddess forbid
he do his own
laundry,
wash his
own dishes,
prepare his
own meals.)

in his eyes,
we shouldn't
have
that much
power
over our own
happiness.

*—our progress scares them & they'll do anything
to put a stop to it.*

how can
she possibly
be a
"gold digger"

if she's
clearly the
motherfucking
gold?

—quickly now.

because you
refuse
to settle
for

a man
who asks
for too
much

& gives
back
far
too little—

because you
refuse
to go to his
bedchamber

where
only
his desires
will be met—

because you
refuse
to bear his
children

& then take
care of them
without any
help from him—

he thinks
you're
taking
away

a toy
that's
rightfully
his.

none
of them
can
conceive that

we now
live in
a
world

where we
no longer
have any
need of them.

—she already has everything she needs
without taking on your needs, too.

can
you
really
call
yourself a
                    good man
if you
willingly
surround
yourself
with the
bad ones
& don't
call them
out on
their
bullshit?

—the answer is no.

they know
their time is up.

they know
their power is

slipping
                    a w a y,

so they're
digging their claws in

to hold on to it
as long as they possibly can.

—desperation has never looked so pitiful.

"when will you stop
acting like such a victim?"

—he screams in her face.

“when will you
 stop making me one?”

—she screams back.

in heels
& in combat boots

the witches
marched forward,

only
to be pushed

hundreds of years
back in time.

—what was it all for?

once, she came
together with
her coven of sisters,

& they truly
believed that they would

magic up equality
for all
womankind,

but you know how
the story goes:

when you arm
a woman
with a fistful of fire,

the world will do
everything

it possibly
can to
unleash

a downpour
over it.

—*gasping for air.*

w
hen
they
throw
you
to the
waves to
prove that
you're a witch,
remember that you can swim.

—coven rule #5.

II. the everlasting flood

she is not angry
about the state of
the world any-
more; she is
simply filled
to the
fucking
brim
with sorrow.

*—but don't worry, the witch doesn't
drown in this one.*

exhausted—
that's what she is.

tired of
fighting against

the mockery
& the violence.

tired of
fighting to be

treated with
basic fucking decency.

tired of
fighting to make

other people
see her personhood.

—she fears this place just wasn't made for her.

if she ran away
to the woods,

would anyone
even bother to
chase after her?

if she climbed to
the top of the
tallest tree & jumped,

would anyone
even hear her?

if she laid down on
the forest floor & let
the moss overtake her body,

would anyone
even notice her?

if no one
posted about it,

would anyone
even care about
what happened to her?

*—women like her don't seem to matter unless
they're dead, & most of the time not even then.*

she longs
to live
among
the wolves.

somehow,
she knows
it would
feel safer

than
walking
alone
through

the city
when
the moon
is out.

*—if she were a wolf, no one
would ignore her howls.*

when i say
"i'm just a girl,"

i'm not
trying to say

that i'm
frail & helpless—

what
i'm saying is

this world is too
un b a l an ced
& overwhelming

for me to
bear any longer.

—just to clear some things up.

it's so difficult

to write poetry
& make art

& find an
ounce of magic

when

everything
that was once good

is now
withering.

—will anyone still like her if her words
don't inspire or empower?

(please don't
think her ignorant—

things have
never been perfect,

but at least
there was some hope,

at least for
a brief moment.)

—wasn't there, wasn't there, wasn't there?

when
she was
just a
little thing,

she
thought
she
could
be
whatever
she wanted
to be when
she
grew up—

a doctor.
a lawyer.
an author.
a princess.
a witch.
a mermaid.

now that
she's a
grown
woman,

she knows
the truth:
she *can* be
all of
those things
(for now),

but
society will
always want
her to be

someone's
wife
or mother,
but
preferably
both—

& just that.

—she can't have everything, even if she does.

"ugh,
can't we
go back
to
when
women
weren't
allowed to
work?"

—she doesn't even know
what she's asking.

"please
do
not
make
us
dependent
on him
again—
please."

*—the centuries of women
before us plead.*

she told everyone
he was dangerous—

a fist through the bathroom door,
a gun on the coffee table.

she told everyone
she was afraid for her life.

when that didn't work,
she took the blame

so he wouldn't
hurt her even more,

& he *still* did;
meanwhile, all they did

was sit back with
some popcorn & watch.

—how too many of our stories still fucking go.

she stands
at the sink
as she rubs
her skin raw,

her greatest
enemy's blood
staining her

right up to
her fucking
elbows.

try not to
jump to
conclusions—

it wasn't a
cheating lover,
nor a jealous friend.

since the day she
woke with blood in
her underwear,

her greatest
enemy of all
has been her
own body.

*—a garbage can filled with tampons
& disposable razors.*

I. three tiny white pills.
II. a small glass of water.

—she can only pray it'll dull her ache,
lest they think her hysterical.

take me
down to
the sea
like they
used to
do with
a
woman
when they
didn't
want to
deal with
her
melancholy
anymore.

—i want to give up on me, too | might as well do it with a good view.

she begged
& begged
& begged

for someone
to help
her

as
she laid
bleeding
on
the marble
floor.

they told her to
smile pretty
for the camera—

over here,
over here,
now over here.

—we'll only ever be cheap entertainment to them.

i would
rather
they
rip me

o p e n

&
take
my uterus
than
tell me
that
i
have
no say
in
whether
or not
i
carry
a child
inside
of
it.

—i would not mourn it, either | i would mourn
only the circumstances that made it necessary.

is there a spell that
will help her forget
what he did to her?

—an inquiring witch.

is there a spell that
will give her a body
he hasn't touched?

—an inquiring witch II.

to her,
nature is
something
sacred,

& she is
a part of
that
nature.

but
she sees
how man
treats the ocean—

forever
filling her
with oil
& waste—

so she
knows that
there is
little hope

that they
will ever
view her life
as

a beautiful,
let alone
sacred,
thing.

something to
protect.
something that
matters.

for now,
she must
live with
the knowledge

that they
will continue
to
treat her

as
something
utterly
replaceable—

a
resource
to damage
until ruined.

—she supposes she really is *like the sea in so many ways.*

apparently
nobody
learned
anything,
so she
was
once again
forced
to watch
so many
people
she loved
& respected
support
a guilty man,

& now
she knows
for certain
that
no one
is
safe.

—i hope you're satisfied with yourselves.

she is constantly
fighting two parts of herself:

I. the one who never
feels feminine enough.

II. the one who knows
she shouldn't give a shit.

—does that make her a hypocrite?
maybe.

if she decides to
embrace her wrinkles

& stop
dyeing her grays,

everyone says
she's "aging terribly."

if she gets
a little bit of filler

& wears
tight outfits,

everyone says
she's "doing too much"—

oh, & she
still looks "terrible."

—i guess if we're not twenty-five,
we might as well perish.

"you wasted
so much
of your youth
by eating
your fill &
not getting
skinny,"

*—said the god sitting on
my left shoulder.*

"you wasted
so much
of your youth
wishing to be
something
other than
what you are,"

—said the goddess sitting on
my right shoulder.

do not
comment
on how
the lady
looks.

she
does not
wish
to be
perceived.

she just
wants to
be invisible
& feel
at peace.

—don't you get it?

no longer
is she
a vibrant
& talented
& shiny

young
woman.

she's old(er)
now,
& people
no longer
find her

as interesting
as before.

she hates
knowing
she only has
a few years
left

to turn it
around

before
the
whole
world
completely

forgets
about her,

walking
past her
like a
chipped but
once-beloved

vase at
the thrift store.

—*her gravestone will read* irrelevant.

she knows
that
she would be
so much
more
successful

if she were
a male writer
capitalizing on
women's
feelings
& experiences,

& it
honestly
makes her
not want
to try
anymore.

*—why does everything have to be
so much harder?*

she stays up
all night
thinking
everyone
she loves is
secretly
sick of her.

she
apologizes
to the trees
whenever
she has to
step on
their roots.

she holds
back tears
whenever
animals
die in
books
& movies.

she's
convinced
that
nothing
she does is
good
enough.

—treat her heart as if it were marked fragile.

i know
how it
sounds,
but

sometimes
i am
so glad
that

i will
not be
bringing
another

girl into
this truly
awful
world.

—she won't have to suffer the way i have.

she
was told
for so long
that

she likes men

that
she fully
convinced
herself

she did.

*—how many parts of her exist just because
someone else said they did?*

it hurts her
to think about

how
long she

thought
her worth

was
directly tied to

a man's
interest in her.

—*compulsory heterosexuality takes*
so much from us.

no woman
should have to

be
afraid to

hold another
woman's hand

out of
the fear that

the wrong
person will see

& neither of them
will walk away alive.

—please don't let our story end in tragedy.

can't
a woman just

open up
a cozy fantasy novel

written by
another woman—

one where
we get to sip tea

in our quaint
little cottages

before tending
to our gardens

& worry not
about a thing—

& become
part of that world instead?

—she just knows it would be so much better there.

why isn't anyone
listening?

stop hurting
innocent people

&

stop burning
important books.

we need them—
every single one of them.

*—on her knees | she sees too many
patterns repeating.*

maybe one day
gaia will awake

from her
peaceful slumber

& see the
pain we're all in

& finally decide
to stop spinning—

let humanity
start over fresh with

a world where
there's only love

for each other
& for mother earth.

—will anything ever be alright again?

she doesn’t
want to
be alone in
her despair.

she wants
to be
surrounded
by her fellow
sisters & siblings.

she wants
them to
comfort her
the way
only they can
comfort her.

—to me, you are a blessing.

when
the world
feels like
a man-made
storm,
be that
calm shelter
for every
woman—
& for every
suffering soul—
you meet
along the
way.

—this is how we survive | the importance of community.

it's
never
too late
to fix
things,

but
in
order
to do
that,

you
cannot
keep
acting
like it is.

—rise to the occasion of never giving up.

as much as she
may want to,
she is not
surrendering.

she will
not *allow*
herself to
surrender.

she might be
breaking d
o
w
n,

but she
knows that she
can build
herself back up

even stronger,
even more
powerful
than before.

—it's okay, she was just on her sad shit again.

sometimes

you must go
backward
in order to move
forward.

sometimes

you must
lose one thing
in order to
gain another.

sometimes

you must bleed
a whole lot
in order to
heal a little.

sometimes

you must endure
the burn of the afternoon sun
in order to enjoy
the midnight starshine.

—you will get through this,
just as you always have.

she doesn't know
where to go from here,

but what
she *does* know is that

she will keep
going, going, going.

if nothing else,

she will
make sure that

the women
who come after her

have plenty of words
that can be used as weapons.

—it's not just about legacy, it's about sisterhood.

after all
the pain
you've
had to
endure,

perhaps
you've
just
forgotten
this, but:

there's
some fight
left in you
yet,
goddess.

—don't forget that ever again.

make them regret
what they have wrought

by thinking they can
ever gain control of us again.

*—never let them rest, witch | make
them beg for our forgiveness.*

make him
stay up
night

after night
after night
after night

wondering
when
you'll

finally come
to exact your
revenge.

make.
him.
sweat.

—show him just as much mercy as he showed you.

pretend to
sink
into the waves
so he thinks
you're
innocent.

play him.

give him
something
to feel
oh-so-chivalrous
about
saving.

then,

at the last
second,
grab hold of
his hand
&
pull him u
n
d
e
r.
only

when his lungs
begin to
f i l l
with water,
ask him,
"how do you fucking like it?"

—turn every table you find.

if you're going to cry, then cry.

once you're finished,
come back to shore & get back
on the battleground.

there is still a war to win, witch.

—coven rule #6.

the time to
come together &
demand change
is always
now.

special acknowledgments

I. *my wife, parker lee*—you were the first person i told when i had the dream about writing this book. you believed it could come true even before i did. thank you for not just keeping my dreams safe but for breathing life into them, & for every coconut mocha latte along the way, of course. <3

II. *my literary agent, lauren spieller*—this was not the poetry collection i initially had in mind, but i just knew i had to write it—thank you for supporting all of my weird little ideas & helping me see them through to their fullest potential!

III. *my beta readers*—thank you, summer, for fangirling about every word i write as well as moderating so many of my events. thank you, christine, for being my rock & my forever cheerleader. you both read the first *witch* so many years ago that sending you *witch II* felt like a fever dream of sorts.

IV. *my friends & family*—to everyone who has supported me along the way, from reposting my poems to venturing out to my events: thank you, thank you, thank you.

V. *my readers*—every day i wake up & think about how grateful i am to have all of you. writing this collection felt like i was tying up loose ends i left for six-plus years. i hope it adds to the first *witch* in a way that's satisfying for you.

about the author

amanda lovelace (she/they) is the author of several bestselling poetry titles, including her celebrated women are some kind of magic series: *the princess saves herself in this one, the witch doesn't burn in this one, the mermaid's voice returns in this one,* & now *the witch doesn't drown in this one.* they also write books about witchcraft & cocreate tarot & oracle decks. when she isn't reading, writing, or drinking a much-needed cup of coffee, you can find her casting spells from her home in a (very) small town on the jersey shore, where she resides with her poet-wife & their three cats.

The authorised representative in the EEA is Simon and Schuster
Netherlands BV, Herculesplein 96 3584 AA Utrecht, Netherlands.
(info@simonandschuster.nl)

Andrews McMeel Publishing
a division of Andrews McMeel Universal
1130 Walnut Street, Kansas City, Missouri 64106

www.andrewsmcmeel.com

26 27 28 29 30 SDB 10 9 8 7 6 5 4 3 2 1

ISBN: 978-1-5248-9004-9

Library of Congress Control Number: 2025943920

Editor: Danys Mares
Art Director: Julie Barnes
Production Editor: Elizabeth A. Garcia
Production Manager: Julie Skalla

ATTENTION: SCHOOLS AND BUSINESSES
Andrews McMeel books are available at quantity discounts with
bulk purchase for educational, business, or sales promotional use.
For information, please email the Andrews McMeel Publishing
Special Sales Department: sales@andrewsmcmeel.com.